An...
Re(... rkbook

Your CBT Guide to Overcoming Fear of Abandonment, Reclaiming Your Worth, and Developing a Secure Attachment Style

Emma Grace

The trademarks that are used are without any consent, and the publication of the trademark is without permission or backing by the trademark owner. All trademarks and brands within this book are for clarifying purposes only and are owned by the owners themselves, not affiliated with this document.

Table of Contents

Introduction

Most of us have the ability to be far happier and more fulfilled as individuals than we realize. Often, we don't claim that happiness because we believe someone else's behavior is preventing us from doing so. We ignore our obligation to develop ourselves while we scheme and maneuver and manipulate to change someone else, and we become angry and discouraged, and depressed when our efforts fail. Trying to change someone else is frustrating and depressing, but exercising the power we have to effect change in our own life is exhilarating.

Robin Norwood, *Women Who Love Too Much*[1]

Life is a constant learning process. Learning takes place in such diverse and mysterious ways that, in many cases, we are not capable of accurately appreciating what is being forged within us. This book is born from within, certainly, but it also pursues a clear objective: to help you, my good friend, who right now is suffering from what you think is an endless horror due to a bad emotional attachment. It's hard I know. I know because I have lived it. And that is why, over the last few years, I have been moved by a series of circumstances that allow me to

---

[1] *Women Who Love Too Much*, Robin Norwood, Pocket; 1st edition.

speak to you with trust and empathy. The first thing I want you to know is that I understand the position you are in and that I do not judge your actions.

However, although life teaches us through painful experiences, they have incredible potential to transform us into better people. And no, I'm not saying it from exaggerated compassion, but from the conviction that everything you're going through today can and should be turned into the launching pad through which your new and improved version will emerge. I know you have everything you need, although right now it's hard for you to understand it. I know that you are a brave and capable woman, who has experienced a deep pain that seems to have no end. I know. You are not alone. Never, under any circumstances, isolate yourself from the world because of pain, even this one that is so strong that it urges you to stay lying in bed.

The book that you have in your hands today is nothing more than the result of many years of training and learning. What I have learned in these years comes from different sources, both academic education and life experience, both unbeatable tools to achieve whatever goal you set for yourself in life. In these pages, you will find recommendations, of course, but also compassion; you will find practical guidelines to redeem yourself from the pain that oppresses your chest, but also empathy; you will find a couple of invitations to self-assessment, but also hugs. Because we are united in the complicity of pain. You should know that everything, even what you feel today, has an expiration date. It is a question of attitude and tools to leave the cell of pain, of attachment, and return to paths where we can love freely and healthily.

For this, I have arranged a fairly simple but powerful thematic structure. In the first chapter, entitled *Different Attachment Styles*, we will address this complex and necessary topic. Here you will learn what are the types of attachments, their possible causes, and some reflections on love as a concept. From now on we will come to the second chapter, *The Anxious Attachment Style*, where we will focus on how this type of attachment affects all the types of relationships that we build in the exercise of life. If you thought that anxious attachment was reduced to romantic love, here you will realize the breadth of its spectrum.

In the third chapter, *Overcoming the Anxious Attachment Style*, we will give a more practical turn to the problem. You will learn to change the attachment style, moving towards a secure attachment that works much better in all kinds of interpersonal relationships. Likewise, we will take stock of false love together and you will learn to build healthy personal boundaries to forge your new version.

Thus we give way to the fourth and final chapter, *Your Healing Routine.* If up until now you thought it was impossible to improve your life, if the feeling that the world is nothing more than limitless horror persists and catches you from the first moment of the morning until the last moment at night, here you will find many recommendations to give that jump that your body, your spirit, and your mind need so much. A jump that will allow you to rediscover your best version, with the vital essence that nests inside every living being. And how? Through a series of practices, you will turn into your new habits.

Each one of the chapters contained in this book has a characteristic that, for me, is essential: validation. Any recommendation, guideline, or suggestion is subject to your own validation. In this way, you will know what works best for you according to your lifestyle and what practices are more suited to your personality and, in general terms, you will thus have a new opportunity to put the pain aside, without repressing it, without ignoring it, accepting it as part of life learning. Because, at the end of the road, it is pain that teaches us the most. Are you ready to join me on this beautiful walk through your personal growth?

Chapter 1
Different Attachment Styles

If you are suffering too much for a person who deliberately left your life, and you interpret their departure as a blow of disloyalty on their part, let me start this book by telling you that you are not alone and that, before making radical decisions, it is convenient to look inward to determine exactly from what position you are generating the affective bonds in your life. As I told you in the introduction, my objective is none other than to teach you some basic concepts of psychology that I have been learning throughout this wonderful journey that we call life. In addition, I have proposed to convert my personal experience and my training into practical, didactic material that will be useful for you to leave this hard moment behind.

But why do we talk about *positions from which we love or positions from which we build ties*? Because, although it is not a secret to anyone, all our interpersonal relationships depend on the type of person we are, with all that this implies. Without developing the ability to look within, and to self-evaluate ourselves, it is practically impossible to determine for sure if the way we love is the right one or if we are trapped in an endless spiral of emotional dependence. The first thing you should keep in mind is that breaking a love bond always brings pain, and that is not subject to doubt. We have all experienced it at some point in our lives!

Based on the aforementioned, it should be noted that all human beings have (to a greater or lesser extent) developed some attachment styles that determine the way in which we relate to the world, in which we read the events around us. Recognizing the attachment style that we have developed is a large part of the healing process that this book will prepare you for. Like you, I was also in a position of deep pain because of a loss. It was only with the passage of time and my interest in human psychology that I realized that a good part of the pain came from an imbalance in my perception of things.

I propose that you take this first chapter as the platform from which we will build a new and improved version of you. You are a valuable and loving woman who deserves to love and be loved in healthy and functional ways. Do not doubt it. However, the path to healing begins by understanding ourselves before pretending that others love us outright. It is not a question of looking for the enemy or of distributing blame, but of accepting our defects and working on them as the creative axis of new and better interpersonal relationships, whether in the loving or interpersonal sphere.

In this first chapter, we will talk about the different attachment styles that we develop from early childhood and the ways in which they work in us. You will learn, among other things, the possible causes that led to this style of attachment. In this way, by accumulating conceptual information, you will get ahead on the journey toward your best version. Are you ready?

Brief Overview of Attachment Theory

The British psychologist John Bowlby was the first professional to face the problems of human relationships from this perspective. His work continues to be considered transcendental and highly valid among the most prestigious professionals in the field around the world. But, in essence, what did psychologist Bowlby tell us? In general terms, attachment theory focuses on the relationships and bonds that people build, including those of the first lineage, such as those between parents and children and romantic partners. However, attachment theory suggests, among other things, that people are born with a certain need to bond with caregivers during the first years of life. If you lived in a home where you enjoyed the presence of your father and mother, these were your caregivers.

The issue becomes more complex when the environmental factors (or the place and the behavioral and/or communication patterns) in which you grew up are not entirely healthy. The result of these early bonds formed with your caregivers can continue to have a marked influence on the bonds you develop throughout your life, regardless of whether we are talking about romantic relationships or interpersonal relationships of different kinds. To know more easily what attachment theory suggests to us, it is necessary to know what an attachment is. It is an emotional bond that we establish with another person. For Dr. Bowlby, the earliest ties have a significant impact on the way we relate to each other as adults. In this sense, he suggested that attachment also has a biological and survival function: to keep the baby close to its mother, thereby amplifying its chances of survival.

At present, there are many studies and investigations that are ongoing to validate or contradict the elementary premises of Bowlby's work. It would not be an easy task, since the currents of thought that differ from Bowlby's work suggest that attachment is a learned process, while he always stressed the vital impulse of children to form bonds with their caregivers. In any case, and regardless of the investigations, the evidence is increasingly in favor of the attachment theory. At the reach of a click, using the power of the Internet, we found dozens of investigations that reached similar conclusions to each other: those children who maintained the proximity of an attachment figure, had a better chance of receiving comfort and protection when they required it. Therefore, more chances of surviving into adulthood.

Among the factors that influence attachment, the following stand out:

- **Attachment opportunities:** When a child is raised in orphanages or by house servants (in short, without the presence of their immediate caregiver), they are more likely not to develop the sense of trust that is necessary to form a healthy attachment.

- **Quality care:** The ideal scenario, is when caregivers are attentive to respond quickly and consistently to the needs of children, helping them learn that they can depend on the people responsible for their care. This trust functions, at the same time, as the essential basis for attachment.

Description of All Attachment Styles and Differences

Talking about attachment theory is not a mere strategy or anything like that. It is essential that you understand the most essential concepts of human psychology so that, in this way, it is much easier for you to extrapolate the information obtained from your own self-assessment. Keep in mind at all times that the basic purpose of this book is to provide you with the tools to identify your attachment style and work accordingly, either to reprogram habits or perception patterns or to strengthen your own ideas for the sake of better interpersonal relationships. Therefore, before moving forward, you must commit yourself to this topic, because we will cover it throughout the next few pages.

Following the premises of attachment theory, there are four elementary styles. Four attachment styles, each with specific characteristics and dissimilar origins, among which you probably find yourself. This does not mean that you should rush to start your therapeutic process (although, on my part, this will always be an unspoken recommendation) or that you should assume that you have lost your sanity and control over your thoughts. Remember that attachments are not necessarily negative, since they are part of who we are and of the immeasurable range of defense mechanisms that human beings develop to guarantee their survival. If I clarify this, it is so that you do not grind every time you read the word attachment. Clearly, there are attachment styles that are less healthy than others and this chapter is, of course, the guide you need to identify the characteristics and differences between each of these.

As you progress with reading, you will realize that each attachment is different, in the same way as its origin. Environmental factors are extremely important in this regard. We talk about probabilities. If a person grew up in a hostile environment, with parents who were not present to attend to the child's security needs, it is likely that they will develop a certain attachment style that will make it difficult for them to relate to the world because they do not feel able to trust in anyone. If, on the other hand, the child grew up with all emotional needs satisfied, they will develop another, much more functional attachment style for adulthood to come. In short, and without falling into reductionism, the factors in which a child grows (and that first bond with their caregiver) will have an undeniable impact on the attachment style that they develop.

That is the fundamental reason why I want to explain to you, step by step, what these attachment styles are about. Thus, beginning the self-assessment exercise that every woman needs to grow as a human being, the time will come to analyze which of these psychological stages you find yourself in according to the attachment theory. It's an arduous process: few people are willing to assume that, even without meaning to, they were part of the problem. But it is the necessary step to improve and grow, dear friend.

Secure Attachment

We will start by talking about secure attachment. As its name indicates, secure attachment is defined by the ability to build healthy, functional, and stable interpersonal relationships. Undoubtedly, secure attachment is considered the healthiest attachment style due to its characteristics. As with the rest of the styles, this one will depend to a large extent on the elements present (communicative, emotional, affective) during the first years of the person's life. That is, the bond created with their first caregivers.

This favorable environment helped them to feel in safe spaces with all the people with whom they create certain affective bonds. They trust and know how to do it. Except for exceptional situations, they will have very healthy romantic relationships because their style of coexistence and relationship is based on trust, a fundamental element in happier and more fulfilling sexual-affective relationships.

These are the main characteristics of a person with a secure attachment style. Take a look and thoroughly analyze each of them:

- Securely attached people experience security and confidence when they are in a relationship with other people.

- Securely attached people feel confident in their abilities to form close, functional bonds. They feel confident in their abilities to navigate through social worlds in a clear, transparent, and effective way. This includes relationships ranging from romantic, friendship, loved ones, family, and work, among others. That confidence allows them to move smoothly through relationships since they move in peace with their own abilities.

- Securely attached people feel confident in their own abilities, and this is wonderful, but their ability to trust other people is even more incredible. They have no problem trusting that the other person will act with empathy, affection, compassion, and understanding. And this tacit trust in the world is what allows them to live relatively calmly in their healthy and lasting relationships.

- Securely attached people are also confident in their abilities to manage stress. Emotional intelligence, developed over the years and relationships with others, is a common denominator in those who have developed this style of attachment.

- People with secure attachments know how to express their emotions with empathy, assertiveness, and clarity. They don't need to run over the other person to let them know that a specific action has hurt them. And this goes hand in hand with their emotional self-control.

- People with secure attachments know how to establish their limits assertively, clearly, and concisely, without this implying offending or hurting the susceptibility of someone else.

This handful of characteristics provides the ideal conditions for good and lasting romantic relationships. When a securely attached person decides to create a bond with someone else, they do so based on what they learned from their first caregivers: they won't hurt me. And that trust, although it seems ironic to say it, gives them the possibility of relating from a much healthier position.

Anxious and Ambivalent Attachment

This type of style is one of the reasons why so many women suffer unspeakably in endless processes of pain and emotional dependence. It is an attachment style that comes, like everyone else, from upbringing. In this case, from an inconsistent upbringing in which the child never felt confident that their caregivers were attending to their needs in real time. The child's needs were not met and this fractured the feeling that they could trust the environment or authority figures. Dad and mom gave variable responses, without generating stability in attention. The fact that they were unpredictable about the emotional needs of children, raises anxiety. If you have to take a look at your childhood to understand some behavior of the present, do it without reproach or doubt.

And it is that confusion was the common denominator during the first years. Among the most outstanding characteristics of adults with anxious and ambivalent attachment styles, the following stand out:

- People with ambivalent anxious attachments are excited and give up quickly when they meet someone. They don't allow themselves enough time for the affective bond to mature in its proper measure, which is why they always jump in search of a safe space that, despite their efforts, they feel never comes.

- People with ambivalent anxious attachments suffer great emotional exhaustion when they get involved and create bonds with others.

- People with ambivalent anxious attachments do everything to try to be the perfect partner, which opens communication gaps and spaces for the other person to misinterpret the whole situation, especially when their attachment style leans more toward narcissistic or detached behaviors. But why do they have this kind of behavior? So that their partners do not abandon them.

- People with ambivalent anxious attachments are hyper-alert at all times. Any small communicative breakdown, any small omission serves to start the machinery of intrusive thoughts. To calm their own insecurity, the person with this attachment style monitors every behavior of their partner or their loved ones.

- People with ambivalent anxious attachments have serious problems setting limits. They have a hard time saying *no*, so assertiveness is rarely on their list of competencies for healthy relationships with others.

- People with ambivalent anxious attachments constantly think that the other person is the center of their universe. They may even neglect aspects of their lives to devote more time and resources (energy, money, attention) to that person as long as they don't leave them.

- People with ambivalent anxious attachments tend to idealize the person with whom they shared the affective bond. They forget their flaws, involuntarily focusing on all the wonderful features of that person.

Avoidant Attachment

Surely you have heard of avoidant attachment. It is a concept that has gained a lot of popularity in recent years, especially when talking about another concept that deserves a lot of debate: affective responsibility. But, in essence, what is avoidant attachment? It is the inability to build lasting affective bonds because the person does not feel comfortable or able to participate in physical and emotional intimacy. We see it in people who tend to behave distant despite the peak of *falling in love* with the other person. They are often confrontational when something compromises their independence and they don't usually give love relationships a name.

This attachment style develops when the child does not have the presence of their caregivers, who leave them alone to fend for themselves, completely ignoring their emotional and/or affective needs. It occurs in an environment where caregivers expect the child to be independent, when they are reprimanded for being dependent, or when the child is reprimanded for verbalizing some emotion.

These are the most important characteristics of people with avoidant attachment:

- Avoidant-attached people persistently avoid emotional or physical intimacy. For them, building a lasting relationship is a real challenge, as they prefer to go one step at a time rather than consolidate the commitment.

- People with avoidant attachment take charge of absolutely everything, independently and without going to their partner or affective bond. Self-sufficiency is the common denominator in these people. In the same way that they do not like to depend on anyone, they flee from anyone who shows signs of dependence.

- People with avoidant attachment do everything in their power to avoid conflict, even going so far as to remain silent. If for some reason, the conflict with their partner is imminent, they will walk away without even giving notice.

- People with avoidant attachment struggle endlessly to understand and adequately express their emotions and/or feelings.

- People with avoidant attachment are very clear about their physical and emotional limits. They are not careful to clarify this issue with their romantic partners, even if this does not favor the dynamics of the relationship.

- People with avoidant attachment feel uncomfortable with displays of emotions that are too deep. When by twists of fate they relate to a person who lives love in the language of words of affirmation, the relationship will explode sooner rather than later, without involving pain for those who have the avoidant attachment style.

Obviously, all these characteristics make it extremely difficult to build healthy and lasting relationships. It is a constant self-sabotage that prevents them from valuing others according to their ways of loving. For people with this attachment style, their independence will always be the highest point of self-realization and tranquility.

Disorganized Attachment

The last attachment style I want to talk to you about is disorganized attachment. This is defined as extremely inconsistent behavior that rarely follows a specific behavior pattern and stems from the difficulty of trusting people. In statistical terms, it is the least likely of those mentioned and develops through a parenting environment where childhood trauma, abuse, or neglect is prevalent both by primary caregivers and other authority figures within the family team. In this sense, the child who grows up in these conditions can see in their caregiver's figures of comfort and fear at the same time, which creates the ideal conditions for an attachment style where inconsistency is the common denominator.

According to recent research, it is believed that this attachment style is associated with much more complex mental health conditions such as personality disorders, substance use disorders, mood disorders, and even self-harm. But how about we take a look at the essential characteristics of a person with disorganized attachment? The following stand out:

- A person with disorganized attachment feels everything very intensely. The smallest of stimuli can trigger a series of reactions that, seem excessive in relation to the size of the stimulus. Whatever the emotion (passion, anger, insecurity) overwhelms them to un-suspected levels.

- A person with disorganized attachment is an extremist. They do not understand nuances: either they are white or they are black. This means that one day they may be able to give up their lives for their partner based on the love they feel and, the next day, hate them with all the strength of their hearts.

- A person with disorganized attachment has difficulty expressing what they feel. Alt-hough they want it with all their might, the intensity of the emotion is so overwhelming that it is difficult for them to express clearly and simply what they are feeling.

- A person with disorganized attachment does not store large amounts of memories about their childhood. If you ask them, they may or may not remember anything at all about certain stages or they may tell you little irrelevant anecdotes to get by.

- A person with disorganized attachment genuinely wants to build a strong and solid affective bond. However, at the same time, there is a deep fear of being hurt and shame at the closeness of the other person.

As you will have noticed, a good part of these characteristics can be explained by the presence of childhood trauma that has taken place during long periods of their childhood. Building a lasting bond with someone trapped in this attachment style is an arduous task because it implies a greater commitment than expected from someone who does not have said attachment.

Possible Causes

Each attachment style occurs under specific conditions, as I explained in each of the previous segments. Regardless of your case, I urge you to analyze your most recurring behavior patterns, the approach you give to your relationships, and the way you manage your emotions when unexpected peaks arrive. The reality is that everything we do and say today, the ways in which we communicate with the environment, can be easily explained through the type of relationship or bond we form with our first caregivers. The attachment theory is increasingly appreciated and valued among the luminaries of psychology, who find in its postulates a compelling reason, an irrefutable argument to explain how attachments are generated during the first years of childhood.

You now know that the relationship you had with your first caregivers is having a big impact on the way you relate to your romantic partners. Avoidant attachment, disorganized attachment, anxious attachment, secure attachment. All these are elements that affect our happiness, especially if we take into account that we are social animals and that the quality of our ties will facilitate the path toward longed-for self-realization. You may not see it today, because pain invades you, because you feel that the person who left you behaved like a real idiot. In fact, it may be that in reality and objectively you have been violated in various ways by your ex-partner; here I will never accept that someone's emotion is minimized. The fact of the matter is that you, too, may have unknowingly contributed negatively to the outcome of that relationship.

I also had a hard time understanding why certain people whom I had loved madly and with incalculable loyalty ended up treating me so badly. It's something I had to deal with for many months due to a divorce and several failed relationships that plunged me to the bottom of a shattered self-esteem. But I began to train myself, I began to investigate and that is how I understood that I myself participated in this dynamic with my attachment style. So both of us, in our ways of loving, were the natural catalysts for the collapse. This does not mean in any way that there are no other people who are responsible for the damage, but it does mean that it is convenient to analyze the situation from a much more pragmatic perspective, moving away from the natural viscerality of a break.

I invite you, then, to look back and analyze what that first bond with your caregivers was like. Were your emotional needs met consistently and on time? Were you required to be independent and rebuked any sign of dependency? They disappeared and were never constant in your needs? Was there some trauma that you probably locked away in some dark corner of your mind? You can seek answers to these questions with a therapist or through an in-depth self-assessment process. In any case, I can assume that with the explanation received so far you have a pretty good idea of what style of attachment you have developed over the years.

Chapter 2
The Anxious Attachment Style

Dependencies are dire from every possible perspective. The chapter that you will read below will serve as a watershed on such a level that it will lead you to question what was that bond from which it was once so difficult for you to get out. If right now you are in the spiral of pain, because you have recently experienced a divorce or because you feel that your relationship is leaking on all sides, attend this reading with commitment and a lot of aplomb. I can guarantee that, in the meantime, you will find more than clear answers about what that relationship that has just come to an end meant. And it is that we do not appreciate things in their proper measure when pain invades us and when it tyrannizes us. Hence the importance of finding tranquility in the midst of turbulence.

As for the content that you will find below, you will know what anxious attachment is about (the most common and harmful in current couple relationships where there is a dependency), how to understand it, how it affects you in all areas of life (work, social, romantic, and family, among others). In short, this second chapter is the origin of the self-assessment that is so necessary to break with the old patterns that are causing you so much damage. Do not give up. You are an incredible, valuable woman who loves madly. Here you will learn why these are positive characteristics and, what is better, the way to regulate what you give for the sake of a longer-lasting connection.

You will learn, among other things, to build healthy personal boundaries, evaluate your old relationship through a more pragmatic lens, and the importance of alternatives such as cognitive behavioral therapy (CBT) or cognitive reframing. We are in this together and I won't let go of your hand.

Understanding Anxious Attachment

If you have ever wondered where this perennial need to be in touch with your partner comes from, the answer may be found in the attachment style that you have developed over time. With attachment theory, which we discussed in detail in the first chapter, we tie up certain loose ends to better understand why certain behaviors, reactions, and thoughts occur. Of course, you now know that the so-called *secure* attachment style works best in the field of interpersonal relationships. Of the spectrum, anxiety is the most common of all and the main reason why so many women suffer seas of pain during the interim and aftermath of their romantic relationships.

While it is true that anxious attachment is very common, especially in parts of the world where dysfunctional families are the common denominator and there is no caregiver figure to validate, respond to, and vindicate the emotions of their little ones in a period of time soon, it is imperative that we move towards a clearer understanding of all the implications that this attachment brings with it.

At the risk of being wrong, I can intuit that the reason you decided to give yourself a chance with this book is that you come from a sentimental breakup that has left you completely devastated and disoriented and has undermined the foundations of your self-confidence. If so, before you continue feeding harmful internal dialogue, continuing to fill yourself with reproaches, why don't you take a few minutes to understand for sure what anxious attachment is all about? You may be surprised to learn that this affects other levels outside of romantic ties.

Now, how does this attachment style manifest itself now that we are adults? There are a series of more or less clear indicators or signals. The most evident of all is the extreme sensitivity to any possibility of being abandoned. Has it happened to you? Do not feel bad if you have experienced this, because it is normal in this style of attachment. Also, don't fall into the trap of thinking you live in a cell to which you don't have a key. You are your own jailer. Therefore, only if you decide will you remain in that dark place. Understanding what anxious attachment is about will be your first step to the freedom that you will build from now on, with my help and your own determination. These are some signs that can help you identify if your prison is anxious attachment:

- You give a high priority to your emotions and act accordingly, sometimes with excessive intensity.

- You feel a deep fear of separation.

- You tend to have serious self-esteem problems.

- For you, it is essential that your partner gives you constant physical contact.

- You are constantly seeking validation from your sentimental partner.

- It is difficult for you to trust the intentions of others, including your romantic partner. This puts you between the sword and the wall: on the one hand, you seek validation from that person; on the other, you distrust any act. Internally, and by living your emotionality with such intensity, you give too much importance to the smallest of gestures, of words. Anxiously attached people, within the framework of couple relationships, live in an everlasting conflict despite the fact that objective evidence does not support their claims.

- They are in a state of alert, which is why they expect the maximum effort from all those with whom they create an emotional bond.

- They are often people who lack emotional intelligence and do not have control over their emotions through reasoning. The explosiveness before the smallest of stimuli is present in them at all times.

- For anxiously attached people, happiness is too steep a slope. It is very difficult for them to achieve a certain balance in their search for happiness due to the lack of trust in others and the intensity of their emotions.

- Following the prison analogy, emotional dependency is the stuff that bars are made of that prevents them from feeling fulfilled at any time.

Now that you've read the unmistakable signs, have you felt identified? It's okay if the matches are high and you feel bad. Remember that you are here to improve your relationship with yourself (internal dialogue) and, as a consequence of this healing process, you will begin to relate to your contemporaries from a new perspective. The fear of abandonment, the scarcity of emotional intelligence. Step by step you will abandon these defects that until today have prevented you from maintaining functional and lasting relationships. You are not in an irreversible situation and it will depend on you and the zeal with which you approach this new point in your existence.

How Anxious Attachment Style Affects All Types of Relationships

When I started this path of personal transformation, I had a hard time understanding that anxious attachment was such a powerful force. In fact, I used to analyze such a concept from a presumptuous and active position. Which is ironic when you consider that I was moving across the full spectrum of pain. The fact that I had such tough romantic relationships, where my attachment would largely determine subsequent events, helped me to be the woman I am today. My intention is the same with you and with all the readers who accompany me from their positions. The anxious attachment style hurts, mutilates, and undermines the quality of life of those who suffer from it to unsuspected levels. Underestimating its implications is not only a basic error but would be the equivalent of leaving a loaded gun on the table under the premise that if no one touches it, the risk is non-existent.

The theme of romantic love, without a doubt, monopolizes the attention. They bombard us with all kinds of stimuli showing us how an emotional dependency ends up destroying the foundations of all romantic affective ties. But is it limited to love? Are the consequences of anxious attachment only present in couple relationships? This is a point that I think is appropriate to address because it means breaking with a myth that is very harmful in modern narrative. As a woman, we are required to perform in many ways. Society is designed in such a way that we are required to be good mothers, ardent wives, excellent professionals, and, at the same time, a series of more or less stereotypical characteristics such as submission, emotionality, and dedication.

Reality has taught us, and this is something that has been widely discussed in the field of sociology and psychology, that the most furious attachments destroy us in every possible way. If, with the information you have acquired so far, you identify that you have many characteristics typical of someone with anxious attachment, this information will be very useful for you to relate to yourself from a healthier position, and, from now on, you will learn to relate much better with your environment and all that this implies.

In the next pages, we will talk about how this style of attachment can affect areas of your life such as your professional development, friendship, going out and meeting new people, among many other spaces that in normal conditions promote a more fluid path towards happiness and self-realization. We will break, eventually, with the myth that for so many years has spread from the cinema, literature, and popular culture. A woman with an anxious attachment style suffers not only from their romantic relationships but from their overall relationship with the world around them. Now does the pain that seems to have settled in the depths of your soul make a little more sense to you? Remember that you are not alone and that all emotional stages are temporary. Starting from this premise, with which you should familiarize yourself, analyze how much or how little your attachment style is currently affecting you.

Workplace

Surely you are wondering how living in anxious attachment can cause you problems in the workplace if you only build superficial relationships there for professional goals. At the beginning of this learning path, I asked myself the same question. I had no idea that a very individual internal mechanism would have a negative impact, especially considering that my co-workers were not people I held in the highest esteem. It was only with the passage of time and the study of attachment theory that I realized that all interpersonal relationships are bonds. For better or worse, there are links in every conversation we have throughout our lives.

Sharing a cup of coffee with a co-worker is enough for various topics of conversation to arise, ranging from the family situation of each one to problems related to work. And in each talk, you are delivering your energy, part of you and what you are. There a bond is built that, even if it is not consciously transcendental, does have a significant presence on a subconscious level. Additionally, it is no secret to anyone that, given the conditions of the world today, we spend more time in the office and sharing with colleagues than at home or in bed with our partner. And that time that we give, that we invest in relating to the rest (even if it is for the sake of a work project) implies a bond.

Having clarified this point, how does anxious attachment affect the workplace? If you paid attention to what you read at the beginning of the chapter, you will have realized that an unmistakable characteristic of anxiously attached people is a lack of emotional intelligence. You will perceive each act/gesture/word with such intensity that your entire psychological skeleton will crumble at an astonishing speed. This, over time, will distance you from coworkers and professional goals, because, for better or worse, in terms of work it is impossible to achieve goals if we do not have the ability to move around all the social scenarios that take place in a working day.

It will be difficult for you to connect if everyone around you has the perception that you are difficult and that your emotionality overwhelms you. This is very important to be clear about, especially if taking strategic positions is part of your plans. It becomes essential that you work on this aspect, your emotional self-control, because in this way you will receive the respect and appreciation that is necessary to climb in the different hierarchies of the world of work.

Friendships

It is said that the biological family works more like an accident than the consequence of our decisions, and it is true. Throughout life, for better or for worse, we build bonds of different intensities that are part of who we are, and that change us as individuals. Later you will learn how the anxious attachment style can and is destroying your romantic relationships, but this is something that also happens with the friends we make over the years. I don't need to give you statistics about it because I bet you've lived in your own skin what I'm talking about.

If you have gone to bed at night wondering why that good friend, who accompanied you for years, suddenly began to gradually separate from you. And although you couldn't find clear answers, those sleepless nights also opened a hole in your soul, in your self-confidence. It's easy, in those moments of vulnerability, to blame ourselves for what happens to us or to spread the blame around without even stopping to think too much about it. But, my friend, the reality is that all people bring with them a universe of conditioning, fears, expectations, and attachments that shape their individual paths. This is a keyword: individuality.

A few years ago a good friend told me that although friendships are broken by specific decisions, these decisions were hardly made with the intent to hurt. And it made a lot of sense to me when I thought about it deeply. Who in their right mind would deliberately choose to hurt someone with whom they shared a beautiful friendship? Nobody. The wounds that arise in friendships (or deep bonds) are nothing more than the result of the attachment styles from which we relate to the world. If you are anxiously attached, you will live everything with a superlative, passionate intensity. But, what if your friend doesn't feel entirely comfortable in this place? Then, step by step, a gap will open up that will only narrow when one of the parties works on their personal healing.

This is why I always advise valuable women who seek my guidance not to take things as a personal attack, especially if that *attack* comes from someone they shared a very close bond with, such as a childhood friend or loved one. It is not a personal attack, but an unmeasured way of defending yourself. Although this can be extrapolated to the field of romantic relationships, we do not spend enough time evaluating how the anxious attachment that governs us has affected the separation of friendships that we considered invaluable in our lives. And this, not taking everything as a personal attack, is a philosophy of life that you would do well to adopt from now on. Understanding, as a concept of emotional intelligence, that each person has their own personal map. That each person has an entire universe inside of them.

Stable Relationships

When we begin to build a romantic bond with someone, we give ourselves inordinately to the emotions that arise there. There is no need to feel guilty about feeling and acting on those feelings. The real problem arises when we are invaded by the idea that there is no happiness outside of that affective bond. It is very likely that you clearly understand what I am talking about. After all, if we agree on these lines, it is because we have both suffered from the impossibility of being with someone or, failing that, from the contempt and pain that invades us when a relationship comes to an end.

You don't have to wonder how anxious attachment can destroy a sentimental relationship because it's something you experienced firsthand. Although it depends to a large extent on the personality of the other person, when our delivery is excessive, we do not have the capacity to calibrate and measure ourselves, to evaluate the other person's reactions to our stimuli. Here the emotion (love) becomes a kind of blindness that prevents us from admiring the whole context from a much broader perspective.

And is that people with anxious attachment do not conceive the single idea of staying away from their love object for too long, which generates an uncertainty that sooner rather than later transmutes into pain.

But what does the other person feel? What does someone who is loved by someone with anxious attachment interpret? A need that goes beyond the normal, the comfortable, and the expected. In general, anxiety is transmitted from one side to the other as if it were a virus, but it does not affect both parties in the same way. While you, who are emotionally dependent on that person, experience any separation intensely, waiting for the moment to be close to your loved one again, your partner fears that your need will grow more and more. The most worrying thing about all this is that the object of attachment, in most cases, does not react with empathy or compassion. Once the straw breaks the camel's back, the attacks and the damages come. It is at this point where we suffer the most because the separation materializes and the feeling that we are navigating in limbo returns.

There is no way for a romantic relationship to last if one of the parties is trapped in a picture of emotional dependency. Sooner rather than later, the rope will end up breaking. Either because the anxious attachment is accompanied by fear of abandonment (that is, the person with dependency will be the one who, out of fear, breaks the ties) or because the object of dependency gets tired of the harassment and the intensity with which the other person expresses their love and their concern for an eventual breakup. To the extent that you begin to work in this direction, making adjustments, and reprogramming your perception of things (of the world and its events), you will learn to communicate from a much healthier and more independent place. So your relationships will be built on more solid foundations.

Dating

Anxiously attached people communicate (verbalization and action) out of deprivation and despair. In simple words, this boils down to the fact that in their minds is the permanent idea of building a bond that is strong enough to withstand the test of time. There are those who do not consider this to be negative, but it will depend on the personality of the person with whom we initiate such a bond. Let's say for example that you just met someone at a social event. He is an attractive man, who fits within your aesthetic preferences. In addition, he behaves according to social norms, something that has always attracted you. He has a good sense of humor, a very cute smile, and is attentive at all times. What does this mean for anyone else? They are mere stimuli without major significance. This is not how the mind of the anxiously attached person works.

For those who live within the anxious attachment, the mere presence of that person is a real challenge, a stimulus that they cannot control. The ability to fantasize about everything they could do as a couple, in the idyllic future, leads them to behave in ways that, far from consolidating the bond, end up breaking it. It is difficult to explain, especially when we are trapped in attachment, how our reactions seem normal inside, but are interpreted by the world as an endless hurricane. And it is true, if we analyze it conscientiously, because what the anxious individual experiences is emotional hunger.

The fact of meeting someone drags us into a process that, under normal conditions, is beautiful from every point of view. When two people meet and express mutual affective interest, new narratives emerge, new communication bridges that purify us from an emotional perspective. There will, of course, be those who are still dealing with conditioning from past relationships. But, in general, terms, that first phase of falling in love is very rich in nuances and textures. It's easy, if you will, to get lost in expectations when everything is flowing as expected.

With anxious attachment, there is no chance that dating will take its natural course. It is then when you want everything and you look for ways to consolidate the bond, even forcibly, even without taking into account what the other person has verbalized about their intentions. It is evident that the situation will get out of hand as soon as the other person notices that there is a need that stands out, that goes far beyond the logical crush of the first weeks. That is why it is essential that you make a floor before running wild in that direction. Going out with someone, and meeting new people is something necessary thanks to the fact that we are social animals. But, good friend, if the anxious attachment is your common denominator, the chances that everything will go well will vanish at an astonishing speed. Either you will sabotage any progress with your attitude, or the other person will go in another direction out of fear of reactive and erratic behavior.

Chapter 3
Overcoming the Anxious Attachment Style

Women (...) have been encouraged from childhood to be dependent to an unhealthy degree. Any woman who looks inward knows that she was never trained to feel comfortable with the idea of taking care of herself, defending herself, and asserting herself. At best, she may have played the independence game, inwardly envying the boys (and later the men) because they seemed so naturally self-sufficient.

It is not nature that grants this self-sufficiency to men; it is training. Males are educated for independence from the day they are born. Just as systematically, women are taught that they have a way out and that someday, somehow, they will be saved. That is the fairy tale, the message of life (...) We can venture alone for a while. We can go to school, work, and travel; we may even earn good money, but underneath it all there is a finite quality to our feelings about independence. Just wait long enough, the childhood story goes, and one day someone will come to rescue you from the anxiety of real life.

Colette Dowling, *The Cinderella Complex: Women's Hidden Fear of Independence.*[2]

In the second chapter, we talk about attachment theory and the four attachment styles with which we relate to the world around us. This information will have helped you to understand more clearly the reason for certain behaviors, feelings, and thoughts related to your previous relationships. From the beginning, I warned you, dear reader, that the information that you would obtain throughout these pages would work as a watershed in your life. And it is that once we understand that we are not bad people, that we are not *harmful lovers*, but that we respond to environmental circumstances that we carry on our shoulders from early childhood, we better understand that we are the consequence of what we have experienced.

Following the line of your cure and what you need to achieve it, we will move forward in this chapter, where we will focus on the anxious attachment style (whose implications you already know) and the importance of overcoming it to make way for the most functional attachment style for your future love relationships: secure attachment. I can tell you here, in this reading, you will face the ghost of your ex-partners from a much more pragmatic perspective.

[2] Colette Dowling, *The Cinderella Complex: Women's Hidden Fear of Independence*. Pocket Books Nonfiction (June 1, 1982).

You will learn to discern if you were really in love or if said bond corresponded more to an affective need that you wanted to solve. We call this balance of false love, and it will be one of the most transformative segments of the chapter.

I won't lie to you about it: this chapter can get hard because it is based on a requirement that you should not let go: take stock of everything you are and what you perceive of yourself. For example, insecurities. It is clear that we all harbor within ourselves all kinds of insecurities that we have acquired over the years. But how do these insecurities affect the way we love or behave in front of the world? Taking the reins of your cure inevitably means grounding yourself, even if you find it uncomfortable or difficult to swallow. I guarantee that your best version will come out of these complex exercises.

For the last segment of the chapter, you will learn everything about cognitive-behavioral therapy (CBT) as a tool to transform your perception from the root. Additionally, the role of self-limiting beliefs from the cognitive reframing approach. The healing process that you need to carry out from now on will require you to attack the problem from all possible positions.

If it's more comfortable for you to start on your own, the next chapter will be your turning point. If you would prefer to receive therapeutic guidance from a professional, on these pages you will learn about the approach of the two most effective therapies to modify your perception patterns. In any case, your resurgence begins now. Pain, like all things in life, has an expiration date. You will learn and discover it on your own and I know that you will do very well.

Switch to a Secure Attachment Style

Throughout my life, I have performed countless work challenges that led me to feel very good about myself. I lived such full moments thanks to my skills and my profession as an environmental engineer, that I came to feel invincible. But then when you least expect it, things and events happen that force you to appreciate life from a radically different view. In my case, it was the experience of the divorce that forced me to ground myself. Surely you have an idea of what it means to live in a relationship where the outcome becomes tumultuous, where the bond is leaking on all sides and we do not fully understand what is happening. I have always said it: divorce is a full stop in the self-improvement of any woman.

At the height of the divorce, when I was still navigating denial about what was happening, I felt my self-esteem shatter, and crumble like a simple cookie. So what could I do? Suddenly my professional successes were not enough because there was something much more valuable that was going to collapse as if swallowed by an immense black hole with its incalculable force. I spent my nights staring into the nothingness of the darkness in my room, recalling anecdotes, wondering if something was wrong with me. Although it was not the first love relationship that was going to the bottom, it was the most important. After all, a divorce is not just anything. I also thought about what I could do to win back that person's love, to make myself noticed. In that desperation you're familiar with, I imagined and did things that I'm not particularly proud of today.

Like mine, there are thousands of similar stories. Stories of extraordinary women who lived through the suffering of separation, coming to mistrust their attributes, their merits, and all those elements that in one way or another make up a person's self-confidence. It was then that I decided, on the advice of some people in my closest circle, to start training in these topics that I am making available to you today. It was that painful experience that allowed me to delve into subjects of human psychology, understanding that it is not always something that one does, but rather what one has always done. And this goes hand in hand with aspects ranging from early childhood to traumatic experiences throughout life.

Today I am fully convinced that the best step to leave that dark place of low self-esteem and pain is to take charge of who we are as human beings. And it's not about (or, at least, it's not the primary purpose) identifying guilty parties in early childhood. There is no use distributing blame on our caregivers for the environmental factors in which we grew up. It is important to identify that, but not to focus too much on things that are beyond our control. In this way, I was able to discern that taking a leap in my attachment style was the logical response to the problems that I had accumulated in my interpersonal and loving relationships. What is more important: I did not do it to recover an old love that has been lost in time, but to recover myself. Such is my purpose with each and every one of my readings. Help them, and stimulate them so that they go from the anxious attachment style to a secure attachment style that is much healthier for relationships.

Take Stock of "False Love"

When a person understands the bond from the anxious attachment style, it feeds a blind tendency to idealization, to fantasy, even when objective evidence does not give way to this type of thought. A simple gesture will be enough for the person to begin to build a series of small fantasies about exaggerated expectations in relation to the bond. The first thing to keep in mind, my friend, is that not all fantasies respond to an anxious attachment style. There are scenarios in which we understand things as they happen, and in these points, the creation of expectations is to some extent understandable. Now, what is the balance of false love in the context that brings us together here?

This could be summed up as the process of discerning if you were really in love with that last person who hurt you so much and for whom it is difficult for you to fall asleep today. The quick and instant answer is: yes. But do you know why this answer is given so quickly? Because we are not programmed to question our own beliefs. Under normal conditions, human beings have the capacity to doubt themselves, but they need to become aware of their fallible nature. Nothing happens if, when doing the exercise, you realize that you were never as much in love as you thought. Trust me, absolutely nothing happens. In fact, you'll likely find that such love was nothing more than a kind of robust endearment that meshed perfectly with your anxious attachment style.

There is bias. What we think we feel is not necessarily a specific emotion, but the conditioning to which we are accustomed or to which we are pushed according to previous experiences. There is nothing wrong with admitting, once discovered, that this *deep love* was nothing more than affection or the need to find someone to cover certain affective deficiencies that we carried on our shoulders. But why is it important to discern this? It is the first step to modifying your perception. In order for us to realize that it was not love in the balance of false love, the passage of time is crucial. Have you noticed that the person you considered your first love no longer has much importance in your sentimental heritage? Because time is clarifying things, it is giving shape to everything.

A good mechanism to apply the balance of false love is to make a list of the positive and negative things that you found in that person. As you carry out the exercise, you will notice that those positive things were nothing more than a reflection of something you needed at that specific moment in your life. Perhaps during years of a tense childhood/adolescence, where traumas or the absence of caregivers prevailed, that first love meant a reunion with secure affectivity. You found in that person a *safe place* that replaced the absence carried over from childhood inside you. This does not mean (not necessarily) that you loved the person, but rather that their virtues (many or few) fit perfectly with your lacks or affective needs.

Take Stock of the Insecurities That Put You in a State of Anxiety (Useless Coping Mechanism)

The reason why a person with anxious attachment suffers excessively lies in the ignorance of their primary insecurities. I understand that it is not at all comfortable to sit down and evaluate those aspects that generate mistrust or that mark us a peak in terms of anxiety, but it is an essential task to cure ourselves of anxious attachment for the sake of a much fuller life. The first thing to keep in mind is that the things that put you in a state of anxiety do not necessarily represent a palpable threat to your physical and emotional integrity. In fact, many times these insecurities are not supported by objective reality. It works more or less as with phobias: irrational fears that arouse a series of signals in the phobic without there being any palpable risk. The clearest example is that of the patient with a phobia of heights, who will be unable to even take an elevator because the physical manifestations of the phobia will arrive.

This does not mean that *all* your insecurities lack support in objective reality, and this exercise seeks precisely to discriminate between logical insecurities and those that are fanciful products of our perception. Hence the importance of carrying out the exercise with complete objectivity and transparency.

We use a sheet of paper and a pencil. You will not need more. You will spend approximately ten minutes taking note of those things that cause you a lot of anxiety in relation to your courtship or marriage. It is completely irrelevant if this list is meaningless or not since the importance of the exercise is to transfer the threat to a tangible scenario. In this case, the paper.

Here are some examples that I have collected throughout my experience helping women with anxious attachment styles:

- The mere idea that my partner is conversing with someone else makes me very afraid. I feel that he will end up abandoning me.

- I don't like the idea of my partner going out with his friends because I immediately think he could use them as an excuse to see someone else.

- It bothers me a lot when my partner doesn't pay attention to the things I say. I instantly think that he has stopped loving me and taking an interest in my things.

- When my partner doesn't call me to say goodnight, I feel like he's no longer interested in me.

- Even when he doesn't say anything to me, silence hurts me, it pushes me to think the worst, that it's a matter of time before he leaves me.

- I feel bad and it irritates me that my partner doesn't make more space in his schedule to spend quality time with me.

Without too deep an analysis, some of these points are totally valid. However, the problem of anxious attachment in couple relationships is not the premise of a certain emotion, but the intensity with which we react to the stimulus. In the previous chapter, you learned that people with anxious attachment have serious difficulties expressing their emotions in a calm and calibrated way (low emotional intelligence and/or assertiveness), so their immediate reaction tends to be anger, and externalized frustration, which always widens the communicative gap with the other person.

Build Healthy Personal Boundaries

To build healthy personal boundaries it is imperative that we hold ourselves in high esteem. Otherwise, we won't even have a notion of where to start.

We've grown up thinking it's okay for people to be unreliable. Even if they are cruel, which also happens with some frequency, or if they are nice. We feed this narrative that the people with whom we share emotional ties must love us yes or yes, regardless of our behaviors or how hurt we are inside. The reality, dear friend, is that people get tired of fighting against a wall. Hence the importance of working on yourself, of recognizing your strengths and how valuable you are, in order to have a clear idea of what limits you are willing to put in the framework of a relationship.

When I talk to you about self-evaluation and self-knowledge, I mean that before going out to find someone who understands you better (so that you feel better loved), it is necessary that you know every little space of your being, of your soul, of your spirituality and your psychology. Understanding for sure what you are willing to allow in a sentimental relationship and, of course, what you would not accept under any circumstances, either because it activates a latent emotionality in you or because it does not add value to what you understand as relational happiness. It is difficult, of course, because you come from an anxious attachment style where the fear of abandonment was your mark, but it is perfectly possible when you propose to look within with objectivity and transparency.

I've learned that people treat you as you let them. Although a good part of the book has gone through the intricacies of internalization, of making ourselves responsible for what happens to us, it is also convenient to keep in mind that there are men and people in general who go through life with little or no empathy. They are often narcissists who have no problem making us feel like the worst human beings in the world, completely ignoring all the sacrifices we make to always be by their side. The fact that we recognize that our attachment style is part of the problem does not take away responsibility for our partner's behavior. Building healthy boundaries is offering a healthy foundation to withstand the flaws of a relationship.

Words, actions, gestures, communicative dynamics. You are an essential part of the relationship. Without you, the table limps; without you, there is no bond. This is something that you have to understand as soon as possible so that you are more capable of setting your limits based on your own emotionality. It is not about conditioning the other person ("You act as I tell you or this is over"), but about letting them know that there are small gestures that hurt you and that you will not allow them, no matter how much you are in love. A man of high value does not beat around the bush in this regard, he has enough affective responsibility to understand your message and generate new dynamics that do not hurt you. The reason? He wants you in his life.

After a Breakup, Don't Jump Into an Instant Relationship

Men and women move, in affective terms, on different paths. A reality that I have faced during this long learning process (both in personal experience and in the experiences of so many colleagues) is that of claiming the famous *one nail drives out another*. How true is this? Undoubtedly, there is nothing more painful than trying to get emotional post-breakup pain from another relationship. It is a basic error that many women commit in the hope of forcibly forgetting the feelings that love failure left in their self-confidence. But it does not work. And it will never work for clear reasons: such relationships never thrive.

They are called bridging relationships because they represent a moment of special vulnerability for women. The passage from one emotional stage to another. If you wonder why bridging relationships never work, it is because of the emotional availability of those involved. Suppose you just got divorced and broke up in a ten-year marriage. It is no small thing: it is a decade of living in the narratives and dynamics of a specific affective bond. If you don't take mourning seriously and decide to jump into a bridge relationship instantly, you will do it out of pain and not out of love. Let's analyze for a moment the specific reasons for this behavior:

- The belief that a new relationship will take us away from the pain caused by separation.

- A lack of empathy and respect for the new person in our lives (who may give their heart to someone who is emotionally unavailable).

- Inability to remain alone, to take care of ourselves without the presence of someone else.

- A superficial need to show your ex that you were able to replace him quickly.

The most fruitful relationships are those that grow in conditions of delivery and reciprocity. Your objective will be to associate with emotionally available people. Your time is worth gold, your energy is worth gold, and your love is worth gold. What's the point of handing it over to the first man who tries to win you over if you're only in the early stages of a duel? Healing is a step-by-step, not a jump from point A to point Z. So the best thing to do at the high point of vulnerability is to reconnect with yourself. Return to those activities that make your heart race, surrender to your personal projects, work on yourself in all possible aspects (emotional, physical, intellectual), and regain, most importantly, the confidence that you are a valuable woman for whom it is worth struggle.

Take your time, you need it, to regain your breath and confidence. It is not a race against time. Even if you consider yourself to be of advanced age, keep in mind that these are social constructs that have nothing to do with reality. There will always be time to create a new bond, but first, you must be sufficiently prepared to move in that direction.

Why Cognitive Behavioral Therapy?

Working on yourself independently will give you results, but it is not always the best alternative. This will depend exclusively on each woman, on her relational situation, and on the emotional and/or affective conditions with which she developed the anxious attachment style. It is important to address all the possible answers so that you, dear reader, have at your disposal a whole range of alternatives to address this problem that today causes you so much pain and a tendency to emotional dependence. And that's how we got to cognitive-behavioral therapy. What is it about? Why has it shown a very high degree of effectiveness in managing affective dependencies?

In short, it is a type of therapy derived from psycho-therapy in which a properly trained mental health advisor guides their patient through a series of sessions. The overall goal of therapy is to help the patient become aware of their vague or negative thoughts so that they are able to visualize demanding situations with clarity. Likewise, it allows the patient to evaluate with the appropriate tools the dimensions of their most common response mechanisms in scenarios of emotional peaks.

Depending on the professional you go to, there are those who can combine CBT with other therapies to treat mental health conditions such as post-traumatic stress disorder or clinical depression. During a CBT session, the health professional will ask a series of questions about your background and how it makes you feel today. Their intention is to accurately identify the way you think, how you interpret emotional events, and how you usually react to them. At the end of the therapy, you will have the necessary tools to question your own negative thoughts and you will know how to react better to the stimuli that used to drive you crazy.

Contrary to what is usually believed, these types of therapies are not invasive at all. There are no reasons to fear. The professional can assign you some small tasks to carry out in the comfort of your home, but the problems that you choose will always be addressed, those that you consider are further affecting your development as a person and your happiness in general.

Cognitive Reframing: Reframing Our Limiting Beliefs

In essence, this type of technique pursues the same purpose as cognitive-behavioral therapy: to change the way we think. Each human being has within themselves a structure of thoughts that has been strengthening or consolidating over the years. A pessimistic person, for example, always moves in these narratives, which is why they are objectively incapable of finding the bright side of a certain event. For them, there are no glasses half full. They are all half empty! Surely you feel identified with this type of thought pattern, right? Let me tell you that the therapies have a great rate of effectiveness in treating these.

However, for cognitive reframing, it is not necessary (or mandatory) to attend a mental health professional who will guide you through a set of therapeutic tools to help you find the root of a problem. In fact, it can be applied on your own if you manage to develop some skills in the basic application of the model. My recommendation, from my own experience and from the testimony of so many women whom I have accompanied in this healing process, is that you lean on someone who has enough experience to help you, to hold your hand during the hard process of changing the way your thoughts move in the face of a negative emotional stimulus.

When you are in front of a trained therapist, there is a sense of security that you do not find when treating yourself independently. Additionally, you will find a professional point of view about the type of beliefs on which they should focus during the duration of each session. One of the keys to cognitive reframing is that it facilitates the understanding of our ways of thinking, encompassing them in the concept of "frames." These frames can be modified and required by the technique as a general part of its purpose. It all boils down to the fact that the patient changes the frame, which means changing and/or modifying the structure of thoughts that pushes them to give too much importance to rather childish events.

A quick internet search will help you find highly trained professionals with the experience you need. However, and this is a recommendation that extends to all areas of mental health, look for references and balance points before scheduling your first session.

Be Aware of Your Protest Behaviors

I know it's hard to look inside and discover that you too have things to improve in relation to certain automatic behaviors that you are not fully aware of. Don't feel bad about it because it is something that happens to all human beings, regardless of whether they are in a loving relationship, missing an ex, or their objective circumstances in general. But, with precise words, what is protest behavior? It is everything we do (every action) that somehow seeks to hurt the other person or transform the living dynamics in the relationship.

The silent treatment is one of those protest actions that we women use the most when we want to win a certain rhetorical battle. If you do a bit of memory, you will surely find several moments in which you implemented the silent treatment with the aim of getting your partner to give in to a certain claim. You should know that this behavior, far from favoring the dynamics of the relationship, widens the gap between those involved. No, dear friend, protest behavior hardly helps to purify the affective bond. Remember this the next time you feel tempted to use a technique for the purpose of manipulating your partner.

- When you feel that your partner is not paying attention to you, do you try to make them jealous with small expressions?

- When your partner does not agree with you on a certain issue, do you look for a way to manipulate him so that he gives in?

- Do you constantly call him, knowing that he informed you that he would be busy with some project?

- Do you constantly check your phone waiting for a notification from your partner?

- Do you stalk him on social media for any sign that he is cheating on you with someone else?

Let's be honest, we've all fallen into these traps. They are behaviors so common that they begin to become normalized, despite the background they entail. Because we don't think about it enough, when we try to make him jealous, we are subconsciously shooting bullets at his safety as a human being. How would you feel in that situation? Affective responsibility is the key. Do not act in such a way that the loved one may feel hurt.

Chapter 4
Your Healing Routine

I bet you've enjoyed each chapter as much as I enjoyed writing them. And although a good part of what I have learned over the years has come from wrong paths, from fostering unhealthy ways of relating to others, today I can affirm with my eyes closed that what I have learned is valuable to me. And it is because it allows me to get closer to other women in a similar position.

Now that you understand what attachment is about, and how emotional dependence is built in a relationship, you objectively accept that it hurts a lot, but that it is not enough to stop us. A few years ago a good friend told me that the most painful love affairs (also living in dependency) had taught her what she needed to know to build the best of all possible relationships with who is now her husband and the love of her life. And this leaves us a clear lesson: going through pain lucidly is essential to obtain the most important knowledge.

You already know the different styles of attachment, the therapeutic recommendations with the highest success rate, and the way in which emotional dependence can destroy everything you are in different areas of your life. But what do we do with all this knowledge? How can we capitalize on this knowledge accumulated during the previous chapters? My proposal is quite simple, as has been the reading in general. In the pages that you will read below, you will find a series of extremely effective guidelines to recover your connection with yourself, the one that many of us lose from the moment a pang of pain reaches our belly and chest.

Throughout this reading, I have opened up to you in many ways. That you have a more or less clear idea of how my path to here was, of everything I had to go through to become this empowered woman and determined to help so many other women who, like me, suffer from the pattern of emotional dependence, it makes me feel confident. So I can be completely honest with you: if you fully comply with the plan that I propose in the next few pages, you will be opening a very important door to improve your relationship with others: the doors of self-perception. Because to the extent that you feel valuable, transcendental again, that you return to the path towards your self-realization without consideration of any kind, from that moment on you will begin to relate to others from a much healthier position. And, after all, that is the idea.

It all starts with the way you perceive yourself, with the type of woman you think you are. I have found that the better we feel about ourselves, the better we will relate to the world around us. I ask you to face the reading of this last chapter with all the determination and openness that you have at hand. I know it will change your life to unsuspected levels!

Avoid Negative Self-Talk

In general terms, internal dialogue is the set of communicative patterns with which we address ourselves. When you get up in the morning and sit in front of the mirror, what is the first thing that comes to your mind? What are those words that are constantly repeated every time you are alone and the conversation is with yourself? This is what we know as internal dialogue. I'll use a couple of examples to better illustrate the idea, okay? Suppose you are in the final stages of college. Soon, if everything follows its course, you will be a professional and you will start your career path. But you lack confidence. You have that taste in your mouth that you are not responsible or attentive enough to take on tasks as decisive as those that come with a position in a company. Then, that perennial distrust will make you question even the most elementary of decisions. If tomorrow you have the opportunity to enroll in two workshops related to your area of interest, and you select one of them, you will reproach yourself for having made the worst decision. That's a keyword: reproach.

Because when your internal dialogue is completely distorted, unbalanced, and conditioned, you don't live in gratitude but in reproach. Your conscious, subconscious, and preconscious minds are hell-bent on finding negative feedback on any path you take, no matter if things went according to plan. Have you felt that? You complain about having studied this or that career, for having chosen this or that position, for going to bed too late, for not having signed up for the gym, for having left your friends alone at the weekend meeting, for paying attention to that man, for getting married, for getting divorced, for not being attentive enough to your ex-partner. It is very hard to feel this, and it puts us in a very painful situation.

Faced with a corrupted internal dialogue, no scenario or action is positive. Do you know why? Because we do not feel in connection with the intrinsic value that lives in us. Even if you stand out as the best student in your college, your subconscious mind will trigger intrusive thoughts in the form of blame; if you get a promotion, if someone validates your intelligence or your leadership, if people who love you deeply surround you. None of this will have the expected effect on your self-confidence because you have not worked on your self-perception. Now, does this mean that we are condemned to live trapped in a string of reproaches that come from ourselves? No. It is possible to moderate your internal dialogue and break, once and for all, with the tendency to interpret everything that happens to you through the lens of pessimism. Here are some strategies and tricks that will help you from now on to transform yourself from the inside out; you are worth it and you deserve it, never forget it.

The First Technique to Improve Your Internal Dialogue: Stay in the Present

Internal dialogue is not only related or happens when we are facing a stressful situation. In fact, most of the time that we unjustifiably recriminate ourselves (filling ourselves with horrible labels that undermine our self-confidence) it is because we are placing ourselves in the future instead of living the present fully and with all the implications that this may have. We overthink in such a way that we stop concentrating on the now. That's when, after an argument, you don't sit down to analyze what could have gone wrong in that talk, but you think about what can happen from now on, how your partner will react, and the possible end of the relationship. It's amazing how deeply this affects us!

Keeping ourselves in the present is, by itself, a method that is used very frequently in techniques and/or channels to strengthen the spiritual bond with ourselves. As human beings, it is time to get rid of the ballast of the future, because it does not exist, and of the past, because there is nothing we can do to remedy what has already happened. Your top priority, to purge harmful internal dialogue, is to live everything with your senses in the now. If right now you feel bad about something that happened, if emotions overflow inside you and you have a lump in your throat, if suddenly your eyes fill with tears and you don't know what to do to feel better, experience each of these emotions and moves on to the next two steps of the segment. I guarantee you will find improvements almost instantly!

The Second Technique to Improve Your Internal Dialogue: Do Not Use Labels

Adjectives are not really useful for expressing discomfort. And this is something that you must understand as soon as possible if you want to change the way you talk to yourself. The most empowered women are those who know how to forgive themselves for mistakes, who know how to understand each other in moments of uncertainty, and who know that they will not always make the best decision. An empowered woman is not one who behaves haughtily as if she lived in a different cloud from the rest, but one who deals with extremely tough situations without losing confidence. It is difficult, of course, it is! But you are here to learn to speak to yourself with affection and without reproaches.

Stop calling yourself stupid, incapable, a bad person, dishonest, disloyal, boring, or unstable. They seem like just words, but harmful adjectives and labels embed themselves in the skeleton of your subconscious and modify it in such a way that it will become customary to react in similar ways when exposed to something that awakens an emotional punch in you. It is not about burying what you feel, because this is impossible, but to stop using your emotion as an excuse and vehicle to exercise violence against yourself.

The Third Technique to Improve Your Internal Dialogue: Talk to Yourself as You Would Talk to a Good Friend

Deep down, internal dialogue is nothing more than a series of communication mechanisms with which you direct yourself. When the situation becomes tough and you are exposed to a stimulus that overwhelms your emotionality, the ideal is that you have the strength to speak to yourself as you would speak to a good friend. Imagine for a moment that your best friend has made a serious mistake at the company she is working for. It is assumed that said error, or omission, could cost her the position if the consequences reach higher ears. In this scenario, what kind of words or expressions would you use to address your friend? Please keep in mind that she feels devastated, that she is afraid, and that she does not stop thinking about her future. So, considering this, your words will be of love and affection. In no way would you dare reproach her for the mistake she made.

Unheard of as it is, it is what you have been doing for all these years. In the face of any mistake, you attack yourself, you reproach yourself, and you question yourself. You communicate with yourself in an unfriendly and unsympathetic way. And that, great friend, is what ends up undermining the foundations of your self-confidence. That is what perpetuates the structure of negative thoughts that today push you to feel less valuable, less important, and less deserving of love. Internal dialogue is reduced to talking to each other well, without hurtful intentions. Consciously, we know it's not okay to beat ourselves up when something goes wrong, but we do. The time has come to change.

From now on, when you feel like something isn't going according to plan, take a breather, do something that gets your heart racing (writing, reading, music, whatever comes to your mind), and use beautiful, powerful, empowering affirmations. Even if deep down you genuinely feel guilty about what happened, stick with the course of the affirmation and you'll be fine. This is told to you by someone who came out of the emotional well that a divorce entails by working on herself through the next point I want to talk about: empowering affirmations.

A Brief List of Affirmations

Have you heard of affirmations? This is a very useful tool. It's amazing how our perception changes when we learn to communicate in self-talk through healthy, trust-filled patterns. For a long time, you have suffered believing that you are not worth enough, that you do not deserve to be loved, blaming yourself for that separation that has you between a rock and a hard place. Although some insist on underestimating the impact of a divorce (or any break in a significant relationship), for those of us who have experienced it, this is a turnaround that can leave us devastated if we do not know how to recover in time.

Ever since I discovered the power of affirmations, I am a different person. I want the same advance for you. But first, what are affirmations? These are small empowering mantras that you will include in your life to reprogram your internal communication patterns. The affirmations have a simple structure (they are sentences, nothing more) that, converted into a habit, rewire the structure of thoughts that we have fed for years and that have been re-powered as a result of the love break. Before moving forward with a list of powerful affirmations that will help you start your own path, keep in mind the following guidelines for the use of affirmations. Are you ready?

- The first thing you should know is that affirmations work as directions. You can easily modify them in such a way that you feel them more genuine and authentic, more linked to your reality.

- When you go to execute your affirmations, try to be in the present tense. May your five senses be in full attention to what you say/express/manifest. Only by being present while practicing the affirmations will you achieve the expected results.

- Several experts in the consolidation of habits agree that it is necessary to carry out an action continuously for 30 days for it to become an automatic response from the subconscious. Stick to the letter, every day, with your affirmations, and you will notice drastic changes in your self-perception.

Now, let's go with some examples of positive and transformative affirmations. All of these proposals are carefully prepared for someone who has self-identified in patterns of the anxious attachment style:

- My feelings are valid.

- If this doesn't suit me, it doesn't work for me.

- I know that [person's name] will always be there for me because I deserve that love.

- I love him too much, but I focus my energy and resources on my personal goals.

- It is healthy and very valid that I depend on my partner.

- I am very valuable in everything I propose within my relationship.

- I am a strong, independent woman who is happy being alone.

- If my current relationship doesn't work out, I will prosper.

- I will not accept anything that is not love, understanding, and respect.

- I know that [person's name] loves and wants me.

- I deserve to have all my emotional and physical needs met.

These affirmations can be modified depending on your reality, your intentions, and your level of maturity. Everything will depend on the emotional state in which you find yourself and what you consider necessary to heal completely. The fact of the matter is that the affirmations should be executed daily, at different times of the day, even if there are no obvious reasons for it because what you get with the affirmations is to reprogram your mind so that there is a healthier thought structure, more functional and more suitable for your new and improved version.

Practice Gratitude

In those moments as hard as a separation, the loss of a loved one, or the feeling that our love is not reciprocated to the same extent, changing the chip of our thoughts is a daunting task, but necessary. Surely you have difficulties falling asleep now that that person is not by your side. You look back and stumble head-on with countless moments in which you had the opportunity to improve, to put yourself as a priority, to demand what you gave, and you are filled with reproaches for having allowed someone else to treat you badly. The nights are especially painful when we live in emotional dependency. The senses, much more acute than usual, seem chrono-metrically coordinated to shoot frames of moments from the past with that person. Surely you have lived it. So what to do in these cases? How does gratitude help us leave these intrusive thoughts behind?

The first thing you should know is that gratitude is not a word, but a philosophy of life. It implies recognizing that many of the things that happen to you bring with their learning, knowledge, and experiences. And, in that case, you focus on what you learned and not on the deep pain that grows inside you like a handful of wild branches. To the extent that you focus all your efforts on assuming what happens to you from a new and empowering position, you will gradually reduce power to those intrusive thoughts that undermine your quality of life. If it hurts, it's because you felt. If you felt it, it is because you are a woman with the capacity to love. It is better to evaluate what we are feeling as if it were a chapter and nothing more.

The book of your life is made up of successive chapters and each one will leave a different moral. In some cases, this moral is accompanied by laughter and merriment; in others, it is accompanied by a lot of pain. If for some reason you have developed one of the attachment styles that were introduced to you since the first chapter, you probably give yourself away with immeasurable force. You want and do everything possible to always be close to the person with whom you build a loving bond. Sometimes this needs for closeness is reciprocated; in others, no. And the pain appears, and with the pain, your internal dialogues are modified. You ask yourself if you are enough if you are really valuable. And you even try to rationalize this feeling: "If I really am valuable, why have my last two relationships ended so badly? Something is wrong with me." The only harmful thing in you is the attachment mechanism, which you developed for reasons that are probably out of your control. Start by being grateful for what you have and what the evidence suggests.

You look around you and find that your loved ones are healthy.

You look around you and find that you have a job that you love.

You look around and find that your friends are meeting their goals.

You close your eyes and find that you are a fully functional woman, without special conditions or breakdowns in your cognitive mechanisms.

And you look around you again and you will find that all the conditions are given for you to breathe the air of life. And you will find food on your table and a roof over your head. And you will also find intelligence and vitality and tranquility and health. We live a life marked by expectations, which pushes us to close our eyes to the little things that are imperceptible to the senses but that are part of our life. Reconnect with that and you will begin to feel more grateful for everything that is around you and within you.

Start a Journal

Since time immemorial, writing has been used as a therapeutic tool. Men and women, from different times and objective conditions, found in writing a practical way to reconnect with the emotional peaks that burned inside them. Although the years have passed and the circumstances right now are diametrically opposite, the reality is that writing remains intact as one of the most wonderful resources that are known in terms of emotional management. If you have doubts about how starting a journal works to heal us from the pain that emotional dependence implies, the simplest explanation is in the subconscious.

Emotions are lodged in the subconscious and we do not have access to them in such a simple way. We need to get involved and commit ourselves in such a way that recognizing emotional patterns, recurring thoughts, and the causes of pain represents a step toward rebuilding our best version. Whatever your current situation, what inflicts your pain, or the reasons why you developed a harmful attachment style, you have every chance to reverse your situation if you know how. The diary proposal helped me a lot when I felt between a rock and a hard place when I was dominated by a hurricane of intrusive thoughts and the feeling that the world was closing in on me.

I'm sure you know what I'm talking about: that moment when the person with whom you shared so many things decides to open up space and move away, despite your crying and your insistence, your reproaches, and the clear demonstrations of suffering. It is there when we question the meaning of empathy, and this comes through an internal dialogue riddled with guilt. "If I was always there for him if I always protected him if I stopped doing things that I was passionate about for him... why does he let me down? Why doesn't he care how I feel?" It is hard to live in our own flesh that we are not loved with the same intensity, but it is also the perfect moment for you to modify your perception of what romantic relationships imply.

When we use a personal diary we use writing to give matter to something immaterial (emotions and thoughts), which facilitates their analysis. It is not necessary to write transcendental ideas in your journal. It is enough that you write how you feel *at that precise moment*, staying in the present. If for some reason you had a bad day, a very strong argument, or you find yourself at that moment in which memories prevent you from staying present, use the journal to describe in detail what you feel with its respective trigger. In general, why is it important? Because by shaping thoughts and emotions, you take them out of the subconscious area. Also with writing you can break down that emotion, taking away its power in your life. I can guarantee you that having started with my personal diary was a turning point in the hard pain processes in which I found myself trapped with my failed romantic experiences.

Relaxation Techniques

There will be no cure if you do not put all your efforts into transforming what hurts you, and what hinders your growth. You may not notice it right now because you are concentrating on remembering the good times of that relationship that has just ended. You may not feel entirely good or in the mood to make small adjustments to your routine. I know what's wrong with you right now. I know that you prefer to stick to a simple routine, to a sedentary way of living because you lack energy and your mood is not the best. However, while I understand the state you're in right now, remember this: it's when we least want to do something that doing it will transform us inside.

Accept my help, which comes from the heart and empathy, for having crossed that same corridor full of darkness that all women with anxious attachment styles who have suffered a love break pass through. It is a corridor that seems to have no end... but it does. And you will find it by your own means! Take this book as a little guide to action. When in doubt, go to these pages and resume from the moment you find yourself. When you don't know what to do or when you need the advice of a good friend, come visit me. You will gladly find me in these words written from love, understanding, and tenderness.

Take action to transform your reality. When we go to the gym, we do it to transform our physical reality and to feel better in terms of health. When we read a good book, we do it to stimulate those corridors of our intellect. On this occasion, the relaxation techniques that I will teach you in the following pages will help you to return to yourself, to reconnect with your essence and with your absolute value as a woman. It hurts, I know, but it's also the best opportunity to show yourself and the world what you're made of. Because you are an incredible woman who will not be defeated. Because you are a woman who will take advantage of the setback (and the suffering) to stand up in your best possible version. How? Join me in these relaxation techniques and find out.

Deep Breathing

The first technique that we will talk about is the so-called Belly Breathing. If you were unaware of this technique up to now, it is quite simple and quite effectively serves the overall purpose of the segment. With belly breathing, you will let go of shallow breathing (the main tributary of anxiety) and learn to breathe more effectively. Its objective is to stimulate the relaxation response of our parasympathetic nervous system. The logical consequence is that anxiety symptoms are reduced.

To carry it out, follow the following steps:

1. Sit or lie down in a position in which you feel comfortable, trying to keep your spine straight.

2. Put one hand on your stomach and the other on your chest.

3. Next, inhale through your nose, paying attention to when the hand on your stomach begins to rise. The hand you left on your chest will remain still.

4. During the exhalation, expel all the air until your lungs have been completely emptied. Just at this moment start a simple inhalation.

5. For the exercise to work best, try to make each breath last an estimated six seconds. If you do several sets, anxiety symptoms, and intrusive thoughts will disappear.

There is also the resonant breath. This technique is much simpler than the previous one, although it will give you the same results: a progressive silence of intrusive thoughts and the disappearance of all the physical symptoms that come from anxiety. And how is it carried out? An exercise so simple that it only consists of two steps:

1. Inhale through your nose for a count of six.

2. Exhale, repeating the process while counting to six.

Repeat the cycle as many times as you wish or until you notice that you are reaching an optimal level of relaxation.

There are many other techniques that start from the same premise, but these two are the simplest. You will be positively surprised at how immediate the results will appear. Use it when you need it, when you consider it necessary, and you will be able to break cycles of emotional reactivity and anxiety.

Yoga

Although in the West there is the idea that the basic objective of yoga is to tone our body, this ancient practice also pursues a more transcendental goal: connecting with our spirituality. And spirituality is a fundamental step to improving ourselves as people, breaking the tendency to anxious attachment and, henceforth, building better interpersonal relationships and affective bonds. This is how Robin Norwood explains it in her book *Women Who Love Too Much*:

> Developing your spirituality, no matter what your religious orientation, basically means *letting go of self-will*, of the determination to make things happen the way you think they should. Instead, you must accept the fact that you may not know what is best in a given situation either for yourself or for another person. There may be outcomes and solutions that you have never considered, or perhaps the ones you've most feared and tried hardest to forestall may be exactly what is necessary in order for things to begin to improve. Self-will means believing that you alone have

all the answers. Letting go of self-will means becom-
ing willing to hold still, be open, and wait for guidance
for yourself. [3]

Now let's get practical. There are many fairly simple
asanas or postures with which you could prepare
an easy routine at home. Before I teach you some,
remember that it's not just about your body. The
greatest benefit you will get from yoga is to clear
your mind and reconnect with your spirituality.

Mountain Pose

1. Stand up on the mat, with your back straight
   and stretched.

2. Open your legs a little so that the feet are
   parallel to the hips. At this moment, your
   arms rest at your sides, without making contact with the rest of the body. Additionally,
   the palms of your hands will point towards
   the thighs.

3. While the head is straight, looking at the
   horizon, begin to lean, rocking from side to
   side very lightly. Let your body weight shift
   from one foot to the other and hold for thirty

---

[3] *Women Who Love Too Much*, Robin Norwood, Pocket; 1st edition.

seconds. Next, rest, supporting the weight on both feet and repeat the exercise.

4. You can start with three repetitions.

Downward Dog Pose

1. This asana begins in a four-legged position on your mat. You must support your toes well because they will give support (along with your hands) to the rest of the body.

2. Take a deep breath.

3. Next, lift your knees off the mat and raise your hips as high as you can. Try at all times to keep the palms of your hands well-supported. If you're looking for a little more stability (I understand you're just starting out), you can take a small step forward with each foot.

4. Hold the position for ten seconds.

5. Finally, lower the hip and return to your starting position. Here, breathing is extremely important. Expel the air from your body and rest.

6. Between three and six repetitions will be enough.

Mindfulness Meditation

This ancient Buddhist practice is another of the best-kept millennial tools to relax and reconnect with our spirituality. Mindfulness meditation has helped thousands of people overcome extremely difficult anxiety, emotional dependence, pain, and mourning. But, without a doubt, the best thing about this Buddhist technique is that it is very easy to apply. Here is a series of recommendations and/or guidelines so that you can start right now to transform your mental reality with relaxation tools.

1. First of all, find a place where you can sit comfortably. It must be a space where there is no excess noise.

2. Close your eyes and focus all your attention on your breathing.

3. Thoughts of all kinds will come. It is unavoidable! Mindfulness meditation does not ask you to suppress your thoughts but to observe them. If one of them comes, watch it and don't judge it. Just watch.

4. You may start to wander in the process. You can allow yourself a few seconds, but as soon as you realize it, bring your full attention back to your breath.

5. Notice any emotions that come up during the duration of the breath.

6. This is the ideal time to purge yourself of corrosive internal dialogue. Therefore, try not to judge yourself in any way while meditating.

7. Make this practice a habit. Dedicate a few minutes each day and do it with patience and commitment. The results will come and eventually, you will feel much better even with those uncomfortable emotions that affected you so much before.

Sports and New Activities

Finally, physical activity will be part of your new healing routine. Once you have understood more clearly how the psychological mechanisms of people with a certain attachment style work, it becomes easier to understand the reason for certain reactions. At this point in the process, you have gotten rid of the need to distribute blame everywhere. You have begun to heal from a much more functional position, and that is the first thing that you must take into account. From now on your top priority is to build the conditions for this healing to be sustainable over time. And, to get to this point, it is essential that you employ new habits that serve to replace any harmful practices that are deeply rooted within you.

Here the key is endorphins. By now, you will know that endorphins are substances that our brain produces and that generate a feeling of well-being and pleasure. Sometimes, due to external factors, the production of this substance is obstructed. It is then that we feel crestfallen, insecure, and unhappy in general. The idea is none other than to facilitate its production through a slight change in our habits. The inclusion of physical exercise, in this sense, will greatly help you so that your brain releases endorphins and gives you that continuous feeling of well-being that is so necessary during a healing process.

If you don't consider yourself a particularly active woman because you lead a sedentary life, including physical exercise may become a bit more of a challenge. Please keep in mind that creating new habits to replace old and unhealthy ones requires a very high level of determination, poise, and willpower. It is when *we least want to do sport* that we must force ourselves to do it. It seems like a contradiction, certainly, but it is the reality of this healing transit that you are immersed in. The happiness hormone is secreted by our brain when we do activities that we like and that are beneficial to us. Even if doing sports is not an activity that you love, your brain will thank you and soon the results will be noticeable, not only on a physical level but also emotionally.

Remember: at this moment when you take a step forward for your well-being, all resources are valid and must be taken into account. It is not a whim. Start with something simple that doesn't put extra stress on you. How about a little exercise routine to do in the comfort of your home? Or, why not define a Sunday outing with your friends to play volleyball in a park? This last option will not only help you because of the sport itself, but also because of the essential contact with Mother Nature.

Sooner rather than later, you will appreciate forcing yourself to spend time doing DIY work and various hobbies that require physical activity. It will be your brain and your soul against the setback that you hope to overcome soon.

Claim Your Worth

The intrinsic value of each human being lies in their ability to become aware of their strengths and opportunities for improvement. In that hurricane of emotions that a love break supposes, self-perception is distorted to unsuspected levels. We reach the point of believing that we will never love again, that we don't deserve a chance in the romantic field, and that we are not enough. This is the worst thing that can happen to us, and it is evident because the reality is that all women have attributes that make them special, regardless of whether they accumulate a series of failed relationships. So how do we claim our worth as individuals?

The best way is to focus all your concentration on activities where you feel in control of the situation. It does not seem easy at first glance, but attitude is essential to choose your battles.

Suppose you just got divorced and you still have the need to keep in touch with that person. This confronts you with a situation that you do not have full control of. You can text your ex, but what will you do when he doesn't reply? Because the fact that he returns the gesture is out of your control. The idea is that you feel in total control of what you do again, and this is only obtained when you expose yourself to moments and circumstances where only you decide what will happen next. Also, doing so requires taking responsibility for your existence rather than handing it over to someone else.

That latent vulnerability in this space that follows divorce or any romantic separation can become a cell. You have to escape from it! And the best way to do it is to take responsibility for yourself. In no way enter dynamics where you are pushed to depend on someone else. Hence the importance of carrying out the routines that we have talked about so far with minimal intervention from your loved ones. You have everything you need to get ahead.

I know that the breakups were not your choice (I understand you better than anyone), that you feed a tendency to self-sabotage, and that you discovered it after the fact. The good news is that you can reverse this situation by getting used to living from and for yourself, even if it means giving up routines that expose you too much to a situation of dependency. Sport, meditation, deep breathing techniques, yoga. May each movement you make in your routine be a decision solely yours!

Take advantage of what you have learned so far and you will do well, you will take certain steps and you will change those corrupted segments of your self-perception. That you deserve to be loved is a reality that you have to reacquaint yourself with. The failure of an affective bond does not determine your human quality, always remember that!

Conclusion

From therapeutic alternatives to the deep self-assessment process necessary to achieve a cure for your pain, all paths were explored in these pages carefully designed to give you functional tools for your current emotional state. Now that you've finished reading, you know that it doesn't make sense to spread blame everywhere, you know that this doesn't help in any way and that everything that happens (even if it hurts), happens for a reason that transcends all of us: learning. The blows of life, for better or for worse, are the unequivocal path to knowledge through experience.

From this journey, you learned that your ways of loving respond, to a large extent, to the style of attachment that you developed during your childhood. An attachment style for which you are not entirely responsible, given that factors beyond your control are involved. Those bonds built with your first caregivers, which we talk about starting in the second chapter, are a clear example of why it is so important to be present in the training of the smallest members of the house. And it is that when we are responsible parents, attentive to the emotional needs of our little ones, we greatly contribute to the type of adults they will become over time.

And, although it is not 100% your responsibility to have developed a certain attachment style, you do have the power to transform this reality now that you are aware of it. Because that pain that invades you and blinds you, that prevents you from sleeping and even eating well, is the broken heart that we all go through at some point in our lives. But, at the same time, a broken heart is a golden opportunity to analyze what we do well or badly in our relationship with others. Since the first chapter, you have been learning amazing concepts, right? Each of them responds to a section that I consider essential in your recovery process.

Decidedly, when we question our patterns to connect with the rest, we discover everything in the path of life. And among the many feasible options, secure attachment emerges as the most functional, healthy, and logical alternative. You already know, good friend, that transforming yourself from the inside out, modifying yourself in the essentials until you build bonds from secure attachment and not from deficiencies or mistrust, is the simplest formula for your relationships to be lasting and happy. Right now it hurts, I know, but there are no excuses. The world does not stop in front of our pain. You have the skills, capacities, and awareness that are needed to make the leap towards a new way of loving that goes hand in hand with your affective expectations.

As logical conclusions to this reading, I leave you the three most resonant.

First: The change lies in you. You cannot take responsibility for how bad some people who did not know how to appreciate the way you loved them made you feel. You cannot take charge of pain and suffering, because there is no way to go back in time to avoid it. What is within your reach is to give your perception a turn of the helm. While the process lasts, and you manage to heal yourself until you reach the secure attachment style, the pain will serve as an indicator that you are still alive. Is there a better gift?

Second: Therapeutic alternatives will always be a good option. If you consider that you lack sufficient self-discipline to transform yourself through the recommendations that you found in the fourth and last chapter, you will have the option of going to a properly trained professional with the necessary experience to guide you in this process. Cognitive-behavioral reframing therapies will help you modify your perception of things, acts, and events. Because therein lies the root of the problem of women who love too much and always get hurt.

Third: Bad experiences do not determine your future. Although today you are suffering the unspeakable because of a series of love failures, later you will find incredible people who will value you and love you according to your needs. The important thing is that you work on yourself, that you prepare enough so that, when that special person arrives, they find your best version. A woman who is already amazing in herself and who, at the same time, has been forged in pain to love from a secure attachment and not from lack.

Thank you for the trust placed in me. I hope and trust that what you have learned in these pages will be useful for you to make the turnaround you expect in your life and in your sentimental relationships. You are an amazing woman! Never forget it! I fully trust that you will find a beautiful love with whom to leverage and grow as a team.

Also keep in mind that if this book has added value to you, and you think it may be valuable to other people, it is a good idea to share information about the book, and recommend that they buy it so they can enjoy the benefits of accessing all the content, and put these tips into practice to overcome all kinds of attachment that may be sabotaging their lives and preventing them from living fully and thus developing their maximum potential.

Thank you in advance for your recommendation.

Made in United States
Troutdale, OR
06/21/2024

20681678R00056